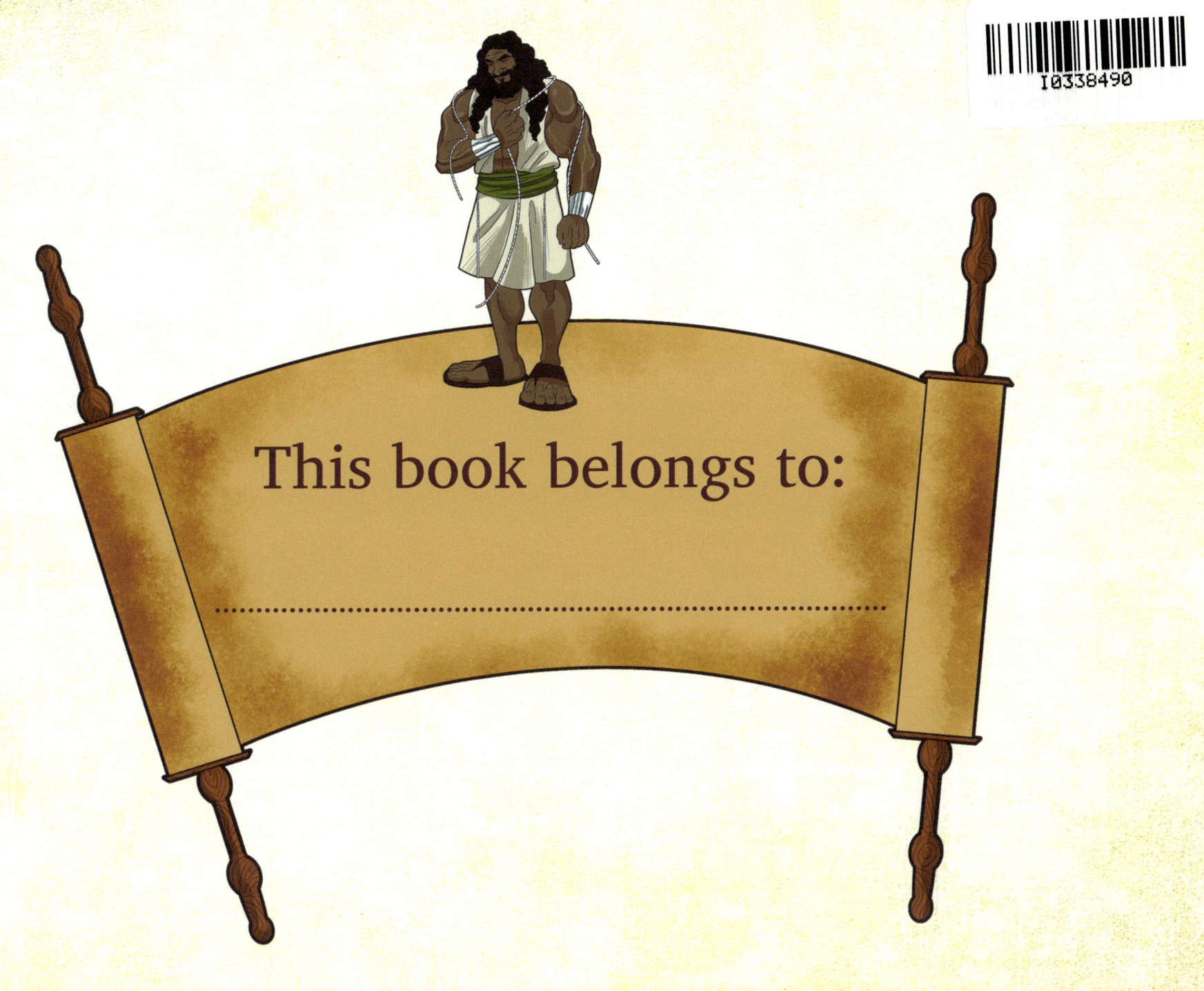

This book belongs to:

....

Copyright © BPA Publishing Ltd 2020

Author: Pip Reid
Illustrator: Thomas Barnett
Creative Director: Curtis Reid

www.biblepathwayadventures.com

Thank you for supporting Bible Pathway Adventures®. Our adventure series helps parents teach their children more about the Bible in a fun creative way. Designed for the whole family, Bible Pathway Adventures' mission is to help bring discipleship back into homes around the world. The search for truth is more fun than tradition!

The moral rights of author and illustrator have been asserted, this book is copyright.

ISBN: 978-0-473-42263-9

Samson: Mighty Warrior

The adventures of Samson

"No razor shall come upon his head, for the child shall be a Nazirite to God from the womb, and he shall begin to save Israel from the power of the Philistines." (Judges 13:5)

When the Israelites began disobeying Yahweh, the God of Abraham, Isaac, and Jacob, He was not pleased. Why couldn't they simply obey His instructions instead of worshipping false gods? He decided to punish the Israelites by sending the fearsome Philistines to oppress them.

The Israelites didn't like the Philistines. They were wicked and cruel, and they liked a good fight. They often attacked the Israelite villages and stole the people's possessions. They made everyone's lives miserable.

But the Father still loved the people of Israel. And He had a plan to save them. That plan included a boy named Samson. He would grow up to be a mighty warrior who would help save the Israelites from the Philistines.

Did you know?

Many people believe there are different ways to pronounce God's name. These include Yah, Yahweh, Yahuah, and many others.

One day, an Israelite woman was busy in the fields when God sent an angel to see her. "Listen!" said the Angel. "Do not drink any wine or eat anything unclean. Soon you will have a baby boy. He will be a Nazarite, a person set apart to serve God. Do not cut his hair."

The woman could hardly believe her ears. She hurried to see her husband, whose name was Manoah. "A stranger came to me," she said. "His face was fearsome like an angel. He said that we will soon have a child!"

"Send the Angel to teach us how to raise this child," said Manoah. And God did so. When the Angel had finished speaking, Manoah fetched a goat and sacrificed it on a stone altar.

Flames from the altar rose high in the air. Suddenly, the Angel shot up into the fire and disappeared. This was no ordinary angel! Manoah and his wife fell to the ground, full of fear. "We will surely die because we have seen God!" they said.

Later that year, Manoah's wife had a baby boy. She named him Samson, just as the Angel had told them. As Samson grew older, he became big and strong. Because his mother had been told not to cut his hair, his hair grew thick and long.

Even though Samson was set apart for God, he didn't always obey Him. One day, when he was grown up, he met a beautiful Philistine woman from the village of Timnah. He said to his father, "I want to marry this girl. Get her for me."

Samson's parents were shocked. God had told the Hebrews not to marry these people or copy their ways. "Why don't you marry a Hebrew girl?" they said. "Why must you marry a Philistine? They have their own customs and gods." But Samson did not listen. "Get the girl for me. I like her," he said. Little did Samson's parents know that God wanted this to happen to create trouble with the Philistines.

Together Samson and his parents set out to meet the Philistine girl and make plans for the wedding. In those days, a wedding feast lasted seven days, so there was plenty to organize! Near Timnah they came to a vineyard bursting with grapes. Because of his Nazarite vow, Samson could not eat or drink anything made from grapes, including raisins and wine. He took a different dirt path than his parents.

Suddenly, a young lion leaped out from the vines. *"RRRRRAAAAGGHHHH!"* roared the lion. It slashed at Samson with its sharp teeth and claws. But the Spirit of God came over Samson and he was not afraid. Using his bare hands, he grabbed the lion and tore it into pieces like a young goat. But he kept it a secret and didn't tell his parents what he had done.

A while later, Samson returned along the same path to marry his bride. When he passed the dead lion, he saw bees had made a hive inside its body. It was filled with delicious sweet honey. He scooped the honey out of the lion and ate it all up. Again, he didn't tell anyone what he had done.

Did you know?

Lions were unclean animals. Nazarites were not meant to touch dead or unclean bodies under any circumstance.

Later that week in Timnah, the wedding celebrations began. Samson's father-in-law invited thirty young men to join them. The musicians thumped their drums and the guests danced and ate until they were full. To pass time, Samson told them a riddle. *"Va yomer lahem me ha ochel yatsa maachal, u me az yatsa matok,"* which meant, "Out of the eater came food, out of the strong came sweetness."

"If you can solve the riddle," said Samson, "I will give you thirty sets of fine clothes. If you cannot solve it, you must give me thirty sets of clothing."

For three days, the young men tried to solve the riddle. But no matter how hard they tried, they could not find the answer. Glaring at Samson's bride, they said, "This Israelite is making us look like fools. Get us the answer, or we will burn down your father's house and you in it."

Samson's frightened bride threw herself in front of him. "You must give me the answer to the riddle," she cried. Samson's answer was no! But after a few days, Samson's ears grew tired of listening to her cry. He gave her the answer, and in turn she told the wedding guests.

The guests laughed all evening at their good fortune. They went to Samson and said, "What is sweeter than honey? And what is stronger than a lion?" Samson's eyes blazed with anger. He knew he had been tricked. "If you hadn't ploughed with my heifer, you would not know the answer to my riddle," he thundered.

The Spirit of God came over Samson again. Flexing his bulging muscles, he marched to a nearby town, killed thirty Philistines, and gave their clothes to the wedding guests. Then he strode back home without his bride. Samson's battle with the Philistines had begun.

Did you know?

At the time of Samson, a favorite party activity was the telling of riddles.

Around the Feast of Shavuot, when the wheat was ready to harvest, Samson went back to Timnah to find his bride. But she was married to someone else. "You ran away, so I gave my daughter to another man," said her father. "Have her younger sister. She's even prettier."

Samson roared in anger. How dare his bride marry someone else! He decided to teach the Philistines a lesson. Catching 300 foxes, he put them in pairs, and tied burning torches to their tails. The foxes raced through the fields in a panic, setting fire to everything in sight. All the wheat was burned to blackened ashes.

When the farmers saw their empty fields, they were furious. "Samson has destroyed our crops," they shouted, "and this is his father-in-law's fault." They found Samson's bride and her father, and burned them both to death. Samson was even angrier than before. He attacked the Philistines in revenge and killed many men. Then he fled to the Israelite town of Lechi and hid in a rocky cave.

Determined to get Samson, the Philistines sent soldiers to Lechi to find him. "Help us capture this brute and we will leave you alone," they said to the Israelites. The Israelites quickly agreed. They were tired of the trouble Samson was causing.

The Israelites knew Samson was big and strong. They sent 3,000 men to the cave to find him. When they reached the cave, they said to Samson, "What are you doing to us? The Philistines are our rulers. We must hand you over to them before you cause more trouble." They tied him up with new ropes and marched him back to Lechi.

As soon as the Philistines saw Samson, they gave a great shout and ran toward him with their swords and spears. But Samson was ready to fight! Tearing the ropes from his arms, he found a donkey jawbone lying on the road and used it to kill a thousand soldiers. The Philistines were no match for the mighty Samson.

For many years, Samson judged the Israelites. Judges were military commanders who made big decisions and helped rule the people of Israel. It was an important job, but Samson couldn't stay out of trouble for long.

One day, Samson went to see a Philistine woman in the city of Gaza. News of his arrival spread quickly throughout the city. "Let's kill Samson in the morning when he leaves," said the people. They surrounded the house where Samson was staying and set a trap for him at the city gate.

Samson knew something was wrong. He jumped out of bed and marched through the streets to the city gate. Using all his strength, he ripped the doors off the gate, threw them onto his shoulders, and climbed to the top of a hill overlooking the city. Samson stood in the moonlight and stared down on the city. "There's no way the Philistines will ever defeat me," he said, laughing deeply.

Sometime later, Samson fell in love with a beautiful Philistine woman named Delilah. When the Philistine chiefs heard about Delilah, they rubbed their hands together with excitement. They knew all about Delilah's wicked ways. "Now is our chance to capture Samson," they said.

Jumping into their chariots, the chiefs sped to Delilah's house to see her. "Next time Samson visits you, trick him into telling you the secret of his strength," they said. "We promise to give you lots of money if you do this."

Delilah's eyes lit up. She liked the idea of earning such riches! She gladly agreed to help the chiefs. The chiefs were happy, too. Even though Samson was stronger than all of them, they knew he loved women very much. They hid inside Delilah's house and waited for their enemy to arrive.

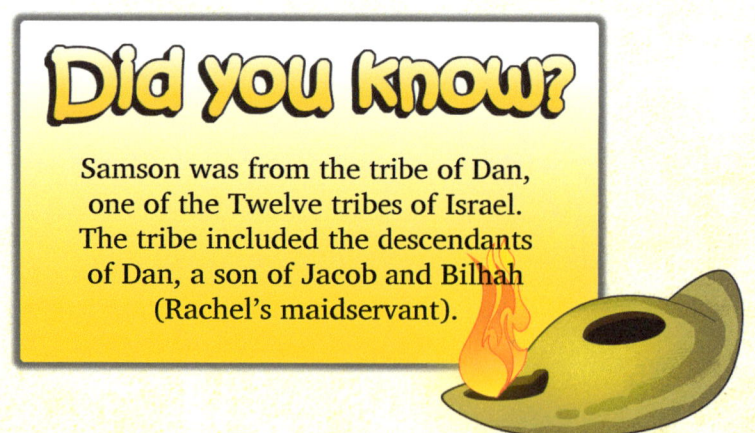

Did you know?

Samson was from the tribe of Dan, one of the Twelve tribes of Israel. The tribe included the descendants of Dan, a son of Jacob and Bilhah (Rachel's maidservant).

The Philistine chiefs did not have to wait long. That night, Samson came to Delilah's house to see her. She curled up beside him and smiled. "Samson, what makes you so strong?" she asked softly. "If someone wanted to tie you up, how could they do it?"

Samson was too clever to be trapped by Delilah. He knew that if he cut his hair, God might take away his strength. He told her a lie, saying, "If you tie me up with seven fresh bowstrings that have never been dried, I will become weak."

When the Philistine chiefs heard what Samson said, they found seven fresh bowstrings that had not been dried. They brought these to Delilah and she tied Samson up with them when he was sleeping. "Hurry! The Philistines have come for you!" she cried. But the Philistines were no match for Samson. He leaped to his feet, snapping the bowstrings like twigs. "This is not the secret of Samson's strength," they muttered angrily.

"You are making a fool of me and not telling me the truth," said Delilah. "Tell me how I can tie you up." Samson lied to her again, saying, "If you tie me with new ropes that have never been used, I will become weak."

As soon as Samson fell asleep, Delilah did just that. "Samson, the Philistines have come for you!" she said. But before the Philistines could grab him, Samson jumped to his feet and broke free from the ropes.

Delilah did not give up. "Do not lie to me," she said, stamping her feet. "If you loved me, you would tell me how to tie you up." Samson's eyebrows shot up. He stared at her suspiciously. "If you weave seven locks of my hair into a loom, I will become weak," he said.

That night, Delilah lulled Samson to sleep. Then she took seven locks of hair and wove them into her loom. "Samson, the Philistines are coming!" she said. "Hurry!" Samson woke from his sleep, pulled his hair loose from the loom, and slipped out of the house. The Philistines fretted and fumed. "This is not the secret of Samson's strength," they said, shaking their fists.

Delilah became even more determined to find the answer. Day after day, she asked Samson to tell her the secret of his strength. Samson grew tired of her bothering him. Finally, he told her the truth. "Because of my Nazarite vow, I have never cut my hair. If you cut my hair, then I will be weak like other men."

Delilah knew Samson was telling the truth. She sent a message to the Philistine chiefs, saying, "Come back one more time. Samson has told me the secret of his strength."

The Philistine chiefs were excited to learn about Samson's secret. They jumped in their chariots and raced to Delilah's house with bags of money. "Now is our chance to capture Samson once and for all!" they cried.

Did you know?

Samuel was a Nazarite. This means he was set apart for God's service. Many biblical scholars believe this is why Samuel never cut his hair.

That evening, after Samson went to sleep, Delilah asked a man to shave off his hair. Then she began teasing Samson. "The Philistines have come for you," she whispered in his ear.

Samson woke up and tried to jump to his feet. But this time he could not break free. His power was gone! The Philistines burst into his room, poked out his eyes, and dragged him away in chains as their prisoner.

Samson became the most famous prisoner in the land. Every day the Philistines forced him to work, grinding grain at the prison. And every night they locked him in a cold empty cell so he could not escape. But slowly, Samson's hair began to grow back.

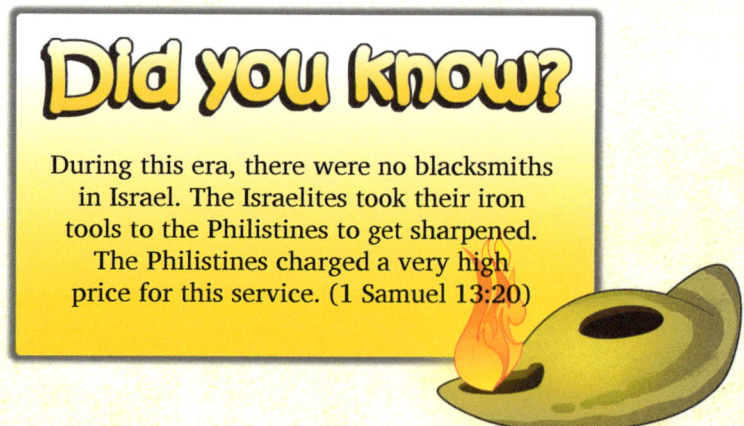

Did you know?

During this era, there were no blacksmiths in Israel. The Israelites took their iron tools to the Philistines to get sharpened. The Philistines charged a very high price for this service. (1 Samuel 13:20)

One day the Philistines gathered at their temple to offer a sacrifice to their fish god, Dagon, and to celebrate their good fortune. "Our god has given Samson into our hands," they said. "Fetch him so that we can mock this Israelite."

Samson was put in front of all the people at the temple. Full of faith, he prayed one last time, "God, give me strength so I can take revenge on the Philistines." Immediately the Spirit of God returned to Samson, giving him great power. Taking a deep breath, he stretched out his arms and placed both hands on the pillars supporting the temple. "Let me die with the Philistines!" he shouted. He pushed against the pillars with all his might.

BOOOOOM! The roof of the temple crashed down in a great cloud of dust. All around was crashing and smashing and breaking. Everyone at the temple, including the Philistine chiefs and Samson, died that day. God had kept His promise. He had used His mighty warrior Samson to free the Israelites from the Philistines.

THE END

TEST YOUR KNOWLEDGE!

(Match the question with the answer at the bottom of the page)

QUESTIONS

Who told Manoah's wife that she would have a son? ....

What important instructions did an Angel give Manoah's wife? ....

What animal did Samson kill with his bare hands? ....

How did the wedding guests know the answer to Samson's riddle? ....

How many foxes did Samson catch? ....

How many Philistines did Samson kill with a donkey jawbone? ....

How many years did Samson judge the Israelites? ....

How much silver did each Philistine king offer Delilah to betray Samson? ....

What happened to Samson when his hair was shaved off? ....

Which Philistine building did Samson destroy? ....

ANSWERS

1. Angel of God
2. Don't drink wine or eat anything unclean, or cut Samson's hair
3. A lion
4. Samson's bride told them
5. 300 foxes
6. 1000
7. Twenty years
8. 1,100 pieces of silver
9. He became weak
10. The temple of Dagon

Complete the Word Search Puzzle

SAMSON
DELILAH
ROPES
PILLARS
TEMPLE

HONEY
DONKEY
PHILISTINE
NAZARITE
HAIR

```
U N Z U T H E D H P
R Z A M K W Z O O P
Z O D Z A P O N N I
H C P E A W U K E L
Y Y M E L R O E Y L
K W O U S I I Y H A
S A M S O N L T S R
T E M P L E W A E S
H A I R K A Z X H L
P H I L I S T I N E
```

Bible Pathway Adventures®

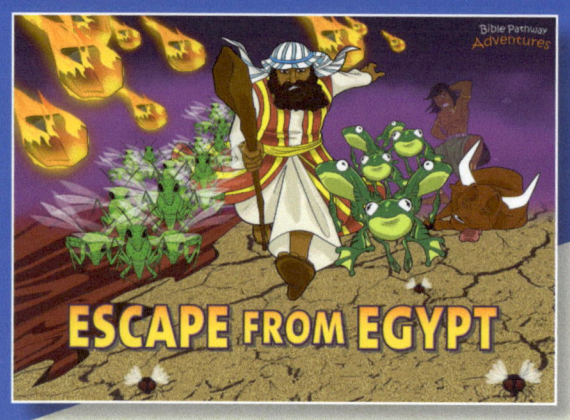

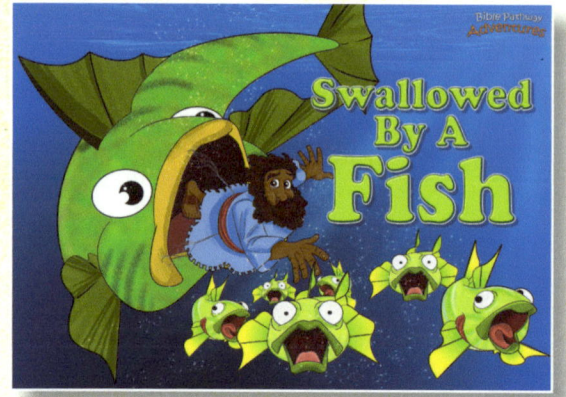

Swallowed by a Fish
Saved by a Donkey
Thrown to the Lions
Witch of Endor
Facing the Giant
Birth of the King
Sold into Slavery
The Chosen Bride
Shipwrecked!
The Exodus
Escape from Egypt
Betrayal of the King
The Risen King

Discover more Bible Pathway Adventures' Bible stories!

Check out Bible Pathway Adventures' Activity Books

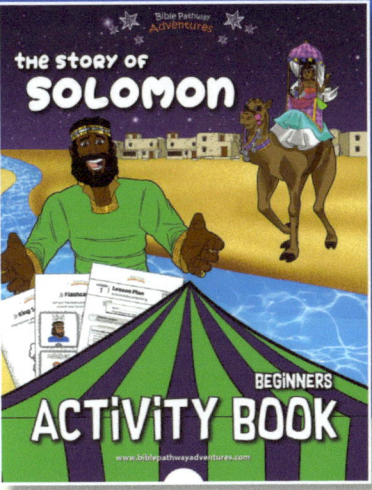
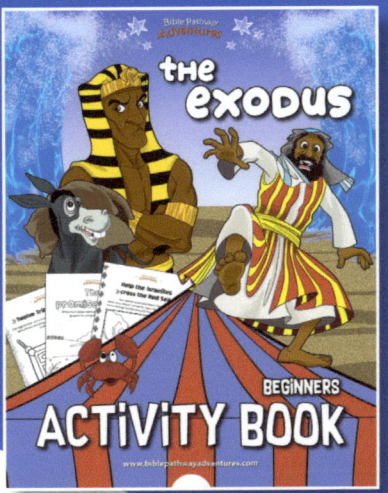

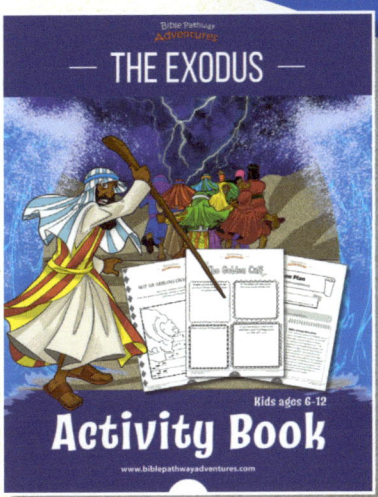

GO TO

www.biblepathwayadventures.com